✿ *Drawing History* ✿
ANCIENT GREECE

Elaine Raphael & Don Bolognese

Scholastic Inc.

New York Toronto London Auckland Sydney

Contents

ISBN 0-590-22729-7

Text and Illustrations Copyright © 1989 by Don Bolognese and Elaine Raphael. All rights reserved. Published by Scholastic Inc., 555 Broadway, New York, NY 10012, by arrangement with the author.

12 11 10 9 8 7 6 5 4 3 2   5 6 7 8 9/9

Printed in the U.S.A.   14

First Scholastic printing, November 1994

Introduction

Can you imagine what ancient Greece looked like?
Today, its beautiful buildings are only ruins; you've
probably seen pictures of them. But 2,400 years ago
these buildings were gleaming marble temples
dedicated to the gods and goddesses of Mount
Olympus. We know about the gods through stories
called myths. In museums we see these gods and
goddesses as they appear in sculpture and on
decorated vases.

In ancient Greece, myths and stories of heroic
deeds were part of everyday life. But the ancient
Greeks were not only exciting storytellers and fine
artists, they were also people with ideas. Many of
their thoughts about mankind, politics, science, and
art are still respected and studied today. That is why
ancient Greece is often called the "birthplace of
Western civilization."

Luckily for us, archaeologists have uncovered the
ruins of palaces, temples, and walled cities of Greek
civilization. Now there is evidence that warriors like
the legendary Achilles and Odysseus really did live
and fight together against the ancient city of Troy.

Can you imagine ancient Greeks in their long,
flowing robes? Can you see the Greek warriors in
their crested helmets? Can you imagine them as they
wait beneath the walls of Troy? They *wait there* for
you to draw them and bring them to life.

Getting Started

This book is a guide to ancient Greek history and ancient Greek art.

The illustrations were influenced by the art on ancient Greek decorated vases. For example, we drew the face of the goddess Artemis (below) in side view because that is how Greek artists usually drew the human face. We also imitated the Greek way of drawing robes.

Ancient Greek vase painters did not use shading or perspective to show depth. However, we used shading in most of our pictures.

For over two thousand years artists have studied and copied Greek art. Fortunately, for us, there are many examples of ancient Greek vases and sculpture in museums. The painting on page 16 is a copy of a vase in the Metropolitan Museum of Art in New York City. If possible, plan a visit to a museum to see the real thing. There are also many fine books on ancient Greece that contain more examples of their art.

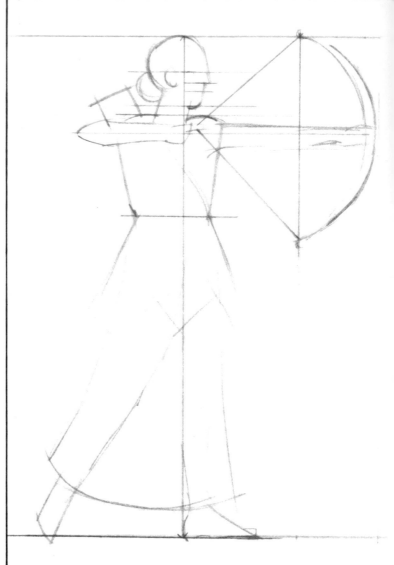

What will you need to do the drawings in this book? Only pencils, paper, and a kneaded eraser. A pad of tracing paper would also be useful.

After you've done some drawings you may want to paint. Any kind of watercolor will do, and at least one small brush for details.

1. Before starting, look carefully at the steps in the drawing lesson above. Note how each step adds to the one before it. Check proportions and guidelines. When you begin, follow the guidelines closely.
2. Are the basic proportions of your drawing like the lesson? If not, maybe you've placed the guidelines in the wrong position.

   When the basic figure looks right, strengthen the outlines. Put in the features with a sharp pencil.
3. Compare your drawing with the lesson. Does something about your drawing bother you? If so—and you can see what it is—correct it. If you can't see what's wrong, put your drawing

away for a while. When you look at your drawing again, check the basic proportions first. If they are all right, look closely at the features. Are they too small, too large, or out of place? After you've fixed what was bothering you, add finishing touches like the decorative stripe along the edge of the dress.

Painting

If you want to paint one of your drawings, first transfer it to heavier paper. Here is a simple way to transfer your drawing: First rub the underside of your drawing with a soft (3B-4B) pencil. Then tape the drawing to the heavier paper. Trace your drawing with a sharp pencil. Now and then, lift a corner to see if the transfer is working.

When you use watercolors, paint the lighter colors first and the darker ones last. Keep the colors clear and bright and use clean water to mix colors. Outline painted areas with a very dark pencil. You can also color your drawings with colored pencils, markers, and crayons.

The Gods on Mount Olympus

The ancient Greeks believed that Mount Olympus, the tallest mountain in Greece, was the home of the gods. From there the gods and goddesses watched over, and often interfered in, human affairs. Zeus was the head of the gods, the most powerful and the most easily displeased. His wife, Hera, was also very powerful and very jealous.

At the moment Zeus is angry with an occurrence on Earth and is about to hurl a few thunderbolts to express his rage.

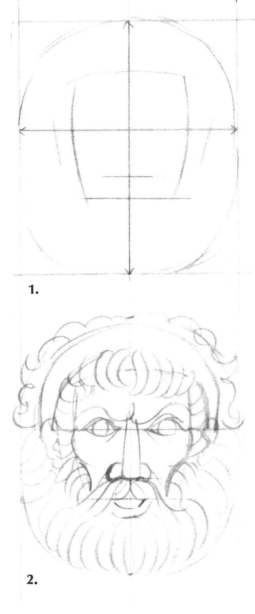

1.

1. **Draw a line down the middle of the rectangle and one across to place the eyes. Add two more lines for the tip of the nose and the middle of the mouth. Then draw the curved outlines for Zeus' hair and beard.**

2. **Put in the main features first. Make sure the eyebrows curve down and join in the middle. This makes Zeus seem angry. Then add Zeus' crown and lightly draw the hair and beard. Don't forget his ears.**

3. **Darken the features, especially the eyebrows and the pupils of his eyes. You can imitate the lesson when drawing the stylized beard or you can experiment and draw it more freely. Finally, add decoration to the crown and tone to the inside of Zeus' mouth.**

2.

3.

The Trojan Horse

The Trojan War was fought during the Mycenaean civilization (about 1600 to 1100 B.C.)—an early period of ancient Greece. Legend has it that a beautiful woman started the war.

Helen, the lovely wife of Menelaus, was kidnapped by Paris, a prince of Troy. Menelaus' brother, Agamemnon, King of Mycenae, was so outraged that he raised an army of Greek warriors. They sailed to Troy and waged war for ten years. In one final attempt to defeat the Trojans, the Greeks tricked them into taking a giant wooden horse into their city.

Here, Greek warriors wait in the shadows. Their comrades, who were hidden inside the hollow horse, have slipped out and opened the gates of Troy. In a minute the waiting warriors will run in, overcome the Trojans, and return Helen to Menelaus.

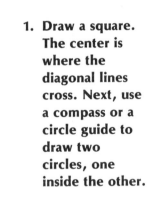

1. **Draw a square. The center is where the diagonal lines cross. Next, use a compass or a circle guide to draw two circles, one inside the other.**

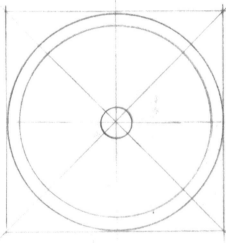

2. **Draw a small circle in the center. Use the guidelines to place the designs. The outer band can also have decoration.**

3. **An example of the mythical creature that was painted on shields. (Place the horse so that the small dot fits over the center of the shield.)**

Odysseus and the Cyclops

For one Greek hero of the Trojan War, Odysseus, the journey home was as dangerous and took as long as the war itself.

In one adventure, Odysseus and his men were captured by a Cyclops—a one-eyed giant who ate people alive.

Here, Odysseus turns away in horror as the giant scoops up one of his men. But soon the clever Odysseus tricks the giant into falling into a drunken sleep. He and his men blind the Cyclops with a sharpened wooden stake. The Greeks then escape by tying themselves to the undersides of the Cyclops' sheep.

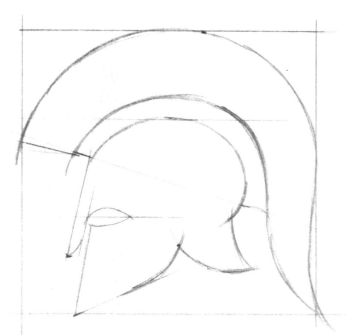

1. **The crested helmet appeared in many variations. This style is one that is often seen on Greek vases. Draw a rectangle that is a little wider than it is high. The two horizontal guidelines show you where the top of the crown and the eye openings go. Sketch the curves of the crest lightly at first. Strengthen the lines when they seem right.**

2. **Add lines to the crest to suggest horse hair. The decorations on the helmet itself can be simple like the example. Add shading to make the crown of the helmet appear to be round. If you wish to try other designs see the painting on the right. Look through books on Greek art for other ideas.**

The Shepherdess

Ancient Greeks believed that every moment of their lives was watched over by the gods. The god Pan, half human and half goat, protected shepherds and their flocks. Here a young shepherd girl looks out over the Aegean Sea. Perhaps she hears some faint music. It might be coming from the reed pipes that Pan is playing, pipes the Greeks believed he invented so that shepherds could use the music to soothe and quiet their flocks.

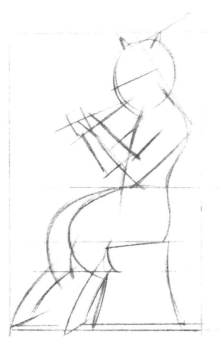  

1. Draw the guidelines for Pan's waist (about halfway up from the bottom of the box). Add two more lines for the top of the tree stump and the bend in the legs. Make sure the angle of the arms and head are like they are shown here.

2. When you are pleased with the figure's proportions, go over the guidelines with curves to make the figure more natural.

3. Draw lines to suggest bark. Add leaves near the stump. Put in small details like fingers with a very sharp pencil.

Athens and the Acropolis

Ancient Greeks built temples to honor their gods. Athens, a city named after the goddess Athena, had its temples on the highest point in the city. This was called the Acropolis and its most beautiful and famous temple was the Parthenon. The Athenians filled the Acropolis with beautiful statues of the gods. Today, the Acropolis is in ruins. Many of the statues that once existed have been taken away and are in museums throughout the world.

Here is one view of the Parthenon as it might have looked. The event is a religious festival and the Athenians are gathering to honor their goddess Athena.

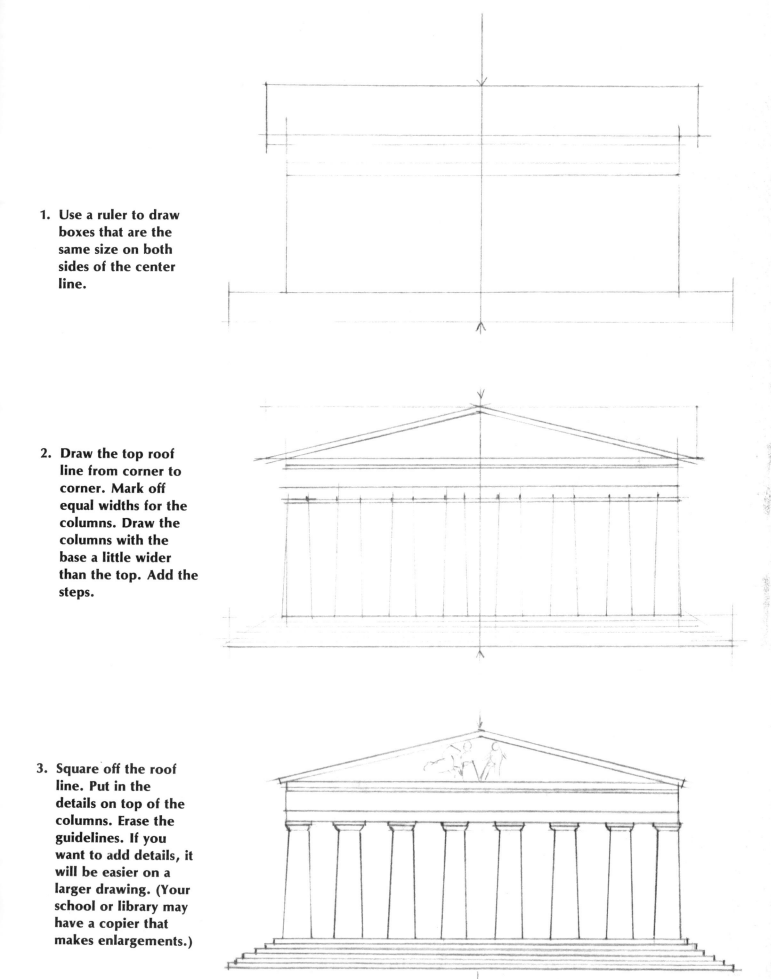

1. Use a ruler to draw boxes that are the same size on both sides of the center line.

2. Draw the top roof line from corner to corner. Mark off equal widths for the columns. Draw the columns with the base a little wider than the top. Add the steps.

3. Square off the roof line. Put in the details on top of the columns. Erase the guidelines. If you want to add details, it will be easier on a larger drawing. (Your school or library may have a copier that makes enlargements.)

Vase Painting

Much of what we know about life in ancient Greece comes from decorated vases such as the jar, or amphora, shown in the foreground. Vase paintings illustrated everyday Greek life as well as stories about the gods and other mythical characters.

The vase painters and the other fine artists of ancient Greece were an honored and respected part of society. Their craft and skills were usually passed on to their children. Here, the painter's son carries a finished kylix—a drinking cup—while his father begins work on an amphora.

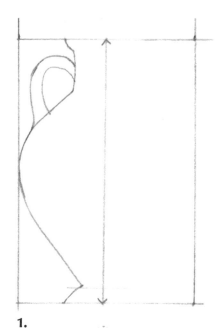

1.

1. **Most Greek vases are symmetrical. Here is an easy way to do a drawing that is the same on both sides. On tracing paper draw a rectangle. Draw a line to divide it in half. Draw only one side of the vase. Fold the tracing paper along the dividing line and trace the outline. This drawing will be on the underside of the paper when it is unfolded.**

2. **Flatten the paper. The two outlines should be exactly the same. Now put clean tracing paper over the first drawing and trace it. Next, add the ovals at top and bottom. Notice that the bottom oval is fuller than the top.**

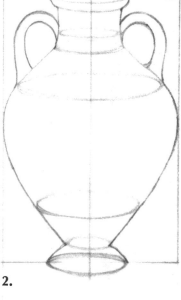

2.

3. **Erase the part of the ovals that you wouldn't see. Add a little shading to emphasize the form of the vase. This fold-over method will help you to draw any symmetrical shape or object.**

3.

Drama in Ancient Greece

Ancient Greeks invented the art of drama. Going to plays was very popular, especially in Athens. The theaters were usually outdoor semicircular arenas called amphitheaters. These were built of stone or wood. Performances sometimes lasted all day. The cast, all men, included a chorus, or group of men, and from one to three actors. The actors all wore masks that stood for the characters they were portraying. Other masks represented gods, goddesses, and emotions like grief, anger, and happiness.

Here, the main character has just discovered that when he was a young man he unknowingly killed his own father. Plays with such dark and tragic secrets were very popular. And some of those same plays are still performed today.

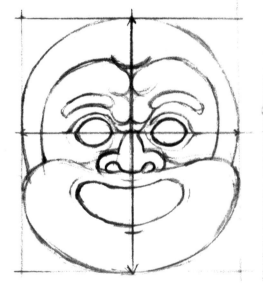

1. **Masks are usually symmetrical. You can use the method described on page 17 to draw these masks. Follow the guidelines for placement of the features.**

2. **Emphasize the eyebrows, nostrils, and mouth. A mask has to express the actor's feelings. Is the actor laughing or crying? Is the play a comedy or does it tell a sad story?**

3. **This mask is for tragedy—stories of horrible events that cause great unhappiness. Notice how the eyebrows, nose, and mouth are different from the comedy mask. Although the details differ, the two masks are basically the same drawing.**

The Birthplace of Democracy

1. **Greek artists enjoyed drawing the graceful curves and folds created by the wearing of a robe. Drawing the line that goes from the floor to the neck will help you to position the feet correctly. After drawing the other straight guidelines, put in the large curves to suggest the robe. The slightly curved lines on the head and face give the impression that the figure is above the viewer.**

2. **Put in the facial features. Draw the arms, hands, and feet. Notice how the speaker's right leg and knee press against the robe (arrow). Observe how closely the robe fits over the left shoulder and arm. Draw the curves on the robe. See how each line forms an edge of a fold at the bottom.**

Athens was a center for the arts. It was also the birthplace of democracy. Other ancient civilizations were ruled by kings, pharaohs, or Emperors. However, Athens in the years between 508 B.C. and 338 B.C. had a form of government called *demokratia*—direct rule by the people. Once every ten days the male citizens (women, foreigners, and slaves were not citizens) met in an assembly called the *ecclesia*. Each man had the right to speak, to propose laws, and to vote.

Here a speaker is urging his fellow Athenians to vote for his proposal. He will be allowed to speak for as long as it takes the water in one jar on the step to flow into the empty jar beneath it.

Athens vs. Sparta

The independent city-states of ancient Greece shared the same language, the same religion and had other similarities. However, two of the greatest cities, Athens and Sparta, were bitter rivals. Each city stood for a different way of life. Athens valued the arts, philosophy, science, and democracy. Sparta glorified the art of war.

Physical strength, fighting ability, and absolute obedience were expected in all the young people of Sparta. From an early age, young boys were prepared to be warriors, and young girls were encouraged to compete in athletic contests. Here a Spartan hoplite, stands his ground, his broken spear at his feet.

1. **Put in the basic guidelines to get the correct proportions. Add the simple shapes of legs, arms, and armor.**

2. **Add curves to arms and legs to suggest muscles. Note how the greaves fit around the shins. The left arm is in position to hold a shield.**

3. **A round shield seen from an angle looks like an oval. After drawing the oval, erase the warrior's left arm and add the design and armor detail.**

Trace your warrior several times to create a row of soldiers.

The Persian War

Only the threat of foreign invasion from people like the Persians could make the ancient Greek city-states unite. In the most important battle of the war, the Greek navy defeated the Persian navy at Salamis, a small island off the coast of Athens. In this battle the Greeks sank 200 Persian ships while losing only 40 of their own.

Here an Athenian boat prepares to ram a Persian boat. The Greek boat is a trireme. It has three banks of approximately 170 oarsmen and carries hoplites and archers. On the bow above the bronze spike there is an eye painted for good luck. A sail was used only in the open sea, never in battle.

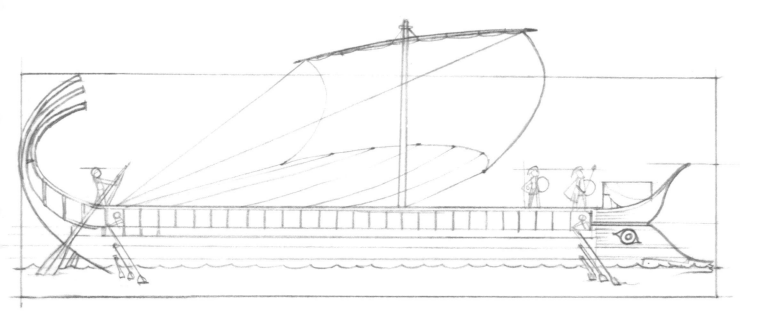

Here only the first and last oarsmen have been drawn. You have to add the others. It would be a good idea to make a large copy of this drawing, because the details will be easier to fill in. Look at the large painting for details of the bow and ramming spike.

The Olympics

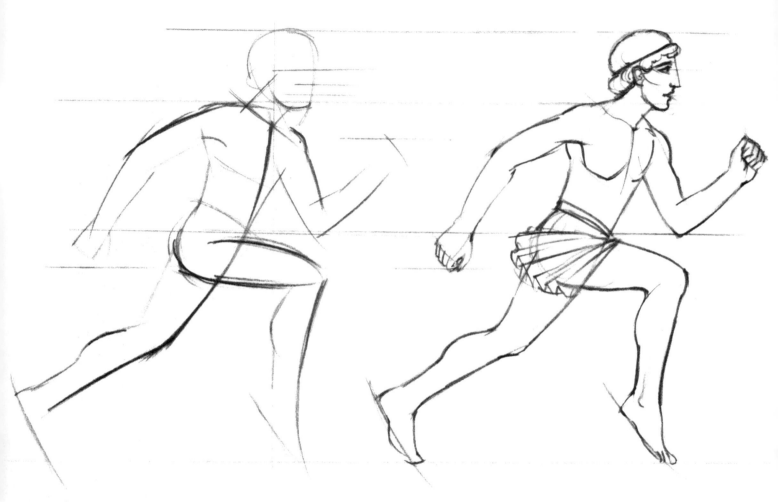

1. **The secret to drawing a figure in motion is to find the main action lines. In this picture one of those lines is the curve that goes from the base of the neck to the knee of the runner's back leg. This and other action lines are drawn with a heavier line for you to see. But when you copy them, draw them lightly.**

2. **Once you have the action the rest is simple. Only a few details are needed to complete the picture. Keep the drawing sketchy to suggest movement and speed.**

Beginning about 775 B.C. the people of Greece began holding athletic games every four years in the city of Olympia. Although rivalries and even wars among ancient Greek city-states were very common, truces were declared during the period of the games so that athletes from all Greek cities could compete without fear.

The runner in this footrace is about to be declared the winner. He will be given an olive wreath and honored throughout Greece. The footrace was the only event for the first fifty years of the games. Gradually other events—the long jump, javelin and discus throwing, and even chariot racing—were added. Our modern Olympics are a continuation of those games, another gift from ancient Greece to us.

Alexander the Great

After many years of fighting among themselves, the city-states of ancient Greece were defeated and united by Philip of Macedonia. His son, Alexander the Great, continued the wars of conquest. In twelve years he carried Greek civilization to all the lands between Egypt and India. People thousands of miles from Athens adopted the Greek language, built Greek-style temples, and imitated Greek art. This period of Greek influence lasted for hundreds of years, even after Rome rose to power.

Here, Alexander watches the burning of a Persian city. Persian captives stand quietly while a Greek soldier examines captured treasure.

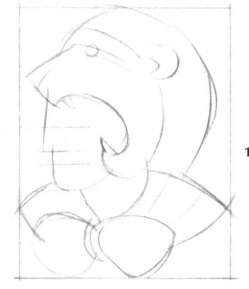

1. **First draw the simple curves of the lion's head. Make sure that the lion's jaws appear to be swallowing the back of Alexander's head. Draw the guidelines for his eyes, nose, and mouth.**

2. **Emphasize the curved eyebrow to give the lion a fierce expression. Alexander's features should be those of a young man.**

Life in Ancient Greece

Ancient Greece was really two civilizations separated by a period of three or four hundred years known as the dark ages. The earlier period, called the Mycenaean civilization, existed from about 1600 B.C. to about 1100 B.C. The archaeologists who uncovered the ruins of Mycenae, the main city, also discovered fragments of a written language. Experts on ancient Egypt also believe that the Egyptians knew the Greeks of this time and traded with them. Many scholars believe that the *Iliad* and the *Odyssey* are stories about warriors from the Mycenaean age.

From 1100 B.C. to 800 B.C. ancient Greece went through a time called the dark ages. During that time the people seemed to lose touch with the rest of the surrounding countries.

Finally, about 800 B.C., the people of ancient Greece became a force again. Their written language was more developed. Their art and architecture had vitality and originality. They began to travel and trade among their neighbors in the Mediterranean area. They gradually became the civilization that has had such a great influence on our lives today.

During that period the city-states of Athens and Sparta became powerful rivals. However, during the Persian invasion (490 B.C. to 479 B.C.) the Greek cities united to defeat the Persians. The next period is often called the "Golden Age of Greece." It produced great works of architecture, art, and drama.

In 431 B.C. Sparta attacked Athens, beginning the Peloponnesian War. The twenty-seven years of war that followed seriously weakened all the city-states of ancient Greece. In 338 B.C. Philip of Macedonia defeated the Greek city-states and united them under his rule. His son, Alexander the Great, went on to invade Persia and extended Greek rule from Egypt to India.

In about 150 B.C. the Greeks were conquered by Rome.

Ionic

Doric

Glossary

Achilles Greek hero of the Trojan War.
Acropolis The highest point in the city of Athens, site of the Parthenon.
Aegean Sea A sea between Greece and Asia Minor.
Agamemnon King of Mycenae and leader of the Greek Army that fought Troy.
Amphora A tall jar with two handles.
Apollo God of the sun, music, poetry, and medicine and a son of Zeus.
Archaeologist A person who specializes in the scientific study of ancient civilizations.
Artemis Apollo's twin sister, goddess of the moon, wild animals, and hunting.
Athena She was born, fully armed, from the head of Zeus; protectress of Athens.
Cyclops A giant with one eye in his forehead.
Demokratia The Greek word for democracy, a form of government run by the people.
Ekklesia The Greek word for ecclesia, meaning an assembly of the people.
Greaves Shin armor.
Helen Wife of Menelaus, King of Sparta, she eloped with Paris to Troy.
Hera Queen of the gods, wife of Zeus, goddess of women and marriage.
Hercules Son of Zeus, and famous for his strength.
Hoplite Heavily armed foot soldier.
Kylix A drinking cup.

Legendary Based on stories and legends.
Macedonia Ancient kingdom just North of Greece.
Menelaus King of Sparta, husband of Helen.
Mt. Olympus Highest mountain in Greece, in mythology the home of the gods.
Mycenae An ancient Greek city.
Mycenaean The civilization which existed in Greece from 1600 to 1100 B.C.
Odysseus An ancient Greek king, and the hero of Homer's epic, the Odyssey.
Pan God of forests, wild animals, flocks and shepherds.
Paris Prince of Troy whose kidnapping of Helen started the Trojan War.
Parthenon Temple in ancient Athens dedicated to Athena.
Pegasus A winged horse of Greek mythology.
Peloponnesus The peninsula of Southern Greece.
Phalanx Battle formation used by ancient Greeks.
Salamis Island near Athens.
Symmetrical Referring to an object or figure whose two halves are exactly alike.
Trireme Ancient Greek warship with three banks of oars on each side.
Trojan Horse A huge wooden, hollow horse inside which Greek soldiers hid.
Troy An ancient city in Asia Minor.
Zeus The supreme god of Greek Mythology.

Corinthian

These are the basic columns used in the buildings of ancient Greece.

Ionic. These columns have capitals with scrolls at the corners. The fluted grooves are rounded at the top.

Doric: This is the oldest and simplest Greek column. The capital is rounded and has no ornamentation. The capitals of all the columns were often painted.

Corinthian: These slender fluted columns are topped by a decorative capital. The leaf forms are based on the acanthus plant.

Index